YOU AND YOUR GRIEF

You
AND YOUR GRIEF

by

Edgar N. Jackson

HAWTHORN BOOKS, INC.
W. Clement Stone, Publisher
New York

YOU AND YOUR GRIEF

Library of Congress Catalog Card Number: 61-18334
ISBN: 0–8015–9036–1

16 17 18 19 20

CONTENTS

A QUIET TALK WITH YOU,   9

DON'T BE AFRAID OF YOUR FEELINGS,   11

THE ROOTS OF GRIEF,   16

WHAT NOT TO DO,   21

HOW GRIEF IS RELIEVED,   26

WHEN GRIEF GETS OUT OF HAND,   29

HOW TO HELP A GRIEVING CHILD,   32

THE FUNERAL,   41

LET YOURSELF BE HELPED,   44

FACING THE FUTURE,   50

RELIGIOUS RESOURCES FOR FACING GRIEF,   55

STRENGTH FOR THE SORROWFUL,   60

YOU AND YOUR GRIEF

A QUIET TALK WITH YOU

I WOULD LIKE TO SIT QUIETLY and talk with you about an event that has left you without the life and love of one who was very close.

I have been with many persons who have gone through this experience. I have been through it myself. I know it is possible to emerge from it.

We have always recognized that grief—the despair and shock you feel now—is one of the most excruciating pains a person can endure. We also know that it is a natural pain, and that the healing power lies within the wound itself. One of the wonders of our minds and bodies is that while scars may remain, most wounds do heal. Grief helps relieve the part of the pain that *can* be relieved, and helps us endure the part that must be endured.

At first you feel that you cannot meet the tasks of even the next few hours. You dread tomorrow and next week. Such fear is natural. But if we find our way through today, tomorrow will be able to care for itself. And somehow, as difficult as it may seem now, the power of life will enable you, as it has helped others, to face death and yet to grow to value life more. You *can* increase your strength. You *can* increase the strength of those who share your loss.

Members of the family—your family—will differ in their reaction to grief. This we expect, since no two of us are alike. If one has always met life's problems with strength and assurance, it is reasonable to assume that he will meet this experience the same way. One who has been easily distressed by circumstances may be so disturbed by the encounter with death that he will need guidance and special help. We hope that this talk with you will also help you to help him and others around you.

DON'T BE AFRAID OF
YOUR FEELINGS

GRIEF IS A UNIVERSAL HUMAN EXPERIENCE. It is the strong emotion we feel when we come face to face with the death of someone who has been a part of our lives.

When we lose forever someone whose life was lovingly and thoroughly enmeshed with ours, we are engulfed by something far deeper than daily, normal disappointments or frustrations. We suffer the loss of love, of emotional security, of a life-sustaining presence. The pattern of our days is shattered beyond recall.

Bereaved persons, faced by this, show their feelings in various ways, and it is therefore difficult to say what is "natural" and what is an unusual expression of grief.

Three doctors I questioned gave different descriptions of the physical symptoms of grief.

One doctor said that grief manifests itself in a state of emotional shock. The person is confused, slow to act, and unable to function in his usual manner.

The second physician said that grief causes an anxiety state. The stability of the person's life has been disrupted, and he is overcome by a gnawing fear that he seems unable to control.

The third physician said that the person in mourning suffers such deep depression that the life processes are retarded, and that he therefore cannot think or act clearly. The physician points out that it is a temporary state and usually does not need special treatment.

If doctors have difficulty diagnosing the way grief affects our bodies, it is easy to see why the average individual can be so confused. The grief you feel may resemble a state of shock, acute anxiety, or deep depression, but it may actually be none of these. Whatever form it may take, it is an emotional state induced by special circumstances, and it has to be dealt with in a special way.

It is good for you to try to understand this now. You may be worried by the waves of intense distress you feel. You may even fear that you will "lose your mind." On the other hand, the death of a beloved person leaves some people absolutely drained of emotion—they wonder why they do not seem to "feel a thing." They worry about this; they think they are "strange." Others react with hysteria. Remember, there are times when it is perfectly normal to act in ways that are not normal for you.

When a person strikes his head, he may "see stars" or be unconscious for a few moments. The cause is clear and the effect is to be expected. When your feelings receive a cruel blow, you may cry, stagger, feel weak and nauseated. You may tremble, shiver or faint. You may find that your emotions are under terribly rigid control, or under little or no control at all. All this is understandable: you cannot have strong feelings without physical effects.

When death comes at the end of a long and useful life, reason and logic, at least—if not our hearts— can accept it, because it is obviously the culmination of the life cycle, and fits into a plan of ordered existence. When death comes because of long illness or advanced age, our minds and our hearts have had some preparation for the event.

But when death comes suddenly or tragically to a child or a youth on the threshold of life, it is different. When a man or woman in full vigor is stricken, we cannot accept it as natural or well-ordered. When a mother dies, leaving young children who need her, we are stunned by the tragedy of it. When a young man who is doing important work for mankind is taken by death, the tragedy is compounded by injustice.

I know something about this. I traveled the battle-fields in wartime, and felt the injustice and brutality of war as I helped to bury many young men who wanted to live but were made sacrifices to man's inhumanity to man. I stood by a small-sized hospital bed and watched life ebb from the body of my son, and felt the unutterable pain of helplessness.

We search for answers when we are forced to face tragic or untimely death. Our reason demands some sort of explanation. It is an impossible task; there are no easy answers, no satisfactory ones. The only answer that could truly satisfy us would be the return of our beloved one, and that we know cannot happen. Our grief is made more poignant by our lack of understanding; it is made sharper by the fact that it was unexpected; it seems more cruel, because when death is sudden or untimely it always finds us in the midst of plans and hopes and dreams that must now be forever unfulfilled.

With such sorrow, we cannot expect to function normally.

You may be unable to eat or sleep. Every task seems too great to tackle. The person who is usually anxious and depressed will be chained by inertia. The energetic person may keep frantically busy, consciously or unconsciously hustling and bustling in an attempt to escape the full impact of his loss. You may feel irritable and "fly off the handle," and then be upset about it. You may want to talk incessantly, or you may want only to be left alone and in quiet. Fearing all loss of control, you may keep yourself under impossibly rigid control. All these feelings are natural.

But when the expression of your feelings is delayed, it may become more difficult and damaging. Sometimes it can take an unexpected form, and be· at first unrecognizable. A study of ulcerative colitis revealed that most of the persons examined had suffered acute grief several months before. Other diseases have also been traced to grief that had turned itself inward, that had not been expressed.

When you are stricken by grief, you are suffering a disease of the emotions caused by facing the reality of death. Slowly, heavily, painfully you learn to let the past go and to turn your mind toward the future. It may at first seem to be a bleak, impoverished future. But it is something you have to bring yourself to accept.

Grief that is not understood, that is forced under the surface, that is not met with compassion, can then show up in disordered behavior, unpleasant physical symptoms, and a disorganized emotional state that may persist for a long time.

Grief that expresses itself naturally, and sorrow that is not suppressed or made into a way of life, allow us to emerge gradually and go on about the important tasks of life—changed, to be sure, but not basically different from the people we were.

THE ROOTS OF GRIEF

*W*HY DO WE GRIEVE? Our reason tells us that the person who has died is free of pain and out of a troubled world. Most religions assure us that death is the advance of the spirit to a better, fuller existence. Many older persons look forward hopefully to death. To those who have been suffering, death is sometimes a welcome release.

Why, then, do we grieve?

There are three major reasons—and to understand them, we have to travel back to our childhood, where feelings take root.

First of all, we grieve for ourselves. If we stop to think clearly and logically—and now, how difficult that may be!—we realize that the person who has died is beyond the problems and feelings of those who mourn his death. So our sorrow is for ourselves. We are sad because we are suddenly, painfully deprived. We ache because we are separated from someone we love and need. We feel this even when we know that death was a release from torment. We feel it even when we admit to ourselves that we would not wish the suffering one back.

Second, there is fear. Our world has changed suddenly, and we do not know what is ahead. That's one fear, and others may stem from the circumstances of this death. Yet perhaps even more frightening are the childhood fears that are sometimes suddenly and terrifyingly awakened. Often adults, without realizing that they are doing it, instill fear of death in a child, making it a dark, horror-filled mystery. "If I should die before I wake . . ." has caused more panic in young minds than most well-meaning parents realize. This fear of the unrevealed future, and the realization that someday each of us must pass into it, does not show on the surface as we grow up. We avoid thinking about it. Then suddenly it is something that happens to someone near and dear to us—and we cannot escape it any longer. The fear that has stayed in the background all these years suddenly comes to the surface and causes panic.

And third, there is insecurity. Insecurity means that the solid earth under your feet is crumbling, and you have nothing to hold on to. This feeling, also, may go back to childhood. The dependable grown-ups upon whose stability our small worlds rested "went to pieces" when death occurred. They cried. They said and did unpredictable things. Our feeling of being secure in their care was shattered; and that insecurity, like fear, grew up with us. So now when death takes a loved one from us, our world totters. The future threatens us. We don't know where the departed one has gone. Order has turned to disorder, and there is no power on earth that can stop it. This feeling of insecurity also shows itself in grief.

What can we do about the fear, the insecurity, the self-awareness that cause our grief?

If life has not taught you this lesson before, you now have been made painfully aware of it: death is as much a part of life as birth and the years of growth. Nothing causes us greater unhappiness, and yet nothing is more certain. With the passing of the years, the physical equipment wears out and the spirit goes on. It would be a difficult thing to imagine a world with no death. In our hearts we may yearn for this, but our minds and our logic reject it. Our earth would be over-populated with sick and ancient and suffering people. Viewed in this way, death is natural. It is not to be feared. It is to be anticipated calmly, as a step in the progress of a person's soul. Even when death is untimely or accidental, when our health and our spirit are strained to the utmost, it still must be regarded as the release of a spirit into a condition where it can find the fulfillment the Creator intended.

To reason this way, over and over until you accept it, helps banish not only your fear of death but also your feeling of insecurity. If you have not found security through faith before death deprived you of someone you loved, you must seek until you find it now. You have prepared yourself for life by accepting certain facts about it. Certain facts must also be accepted about death—above all the in-evitability of it. It is part of the order of things for all of us, and in acknowledging that truth lies your security.

As for the part of your grief caused by your own tremendous sense of deprivation, perhaps you can meet it better if you think about how you adjusted yourself to other losses. If, as a child, you were "given into" at every point, you had little early experience in handling disappointments. If you learned to ac-cept losses and if you were wisely taught that you could not always "have your own way," then it became more possible for you to face major disap-pointments. We can never master our feelings until we truly understand them.

Take time now to ask yourself why you are grieving. Reason tells you that you need not fear death. Reason tells you that death is part of the natural order and will not shatter your world. Reason tells you that the loved one is beyond pain and that you are grieving primarily for yourself. You may not understand this at once. But think of it again and again. Eventually you will feel the heal-ing process begin. But first you must experience the pain of realization.

WHAT NOT TO DO

DON'T CONDEMN YOURSELF. It is natural to say, "If only I had called the doctor sooner," or "If I had only not said some of the things I said," or "If only I had known."

Most of us have such feelings of self-judgment and guilt after we have lost someone who was close to us. Those nagging doubts and recriminations grow from any close relationship with another person. But no one can foresee all that may happen, and no one can go through life doing everything possible to meet every possible turn and twist and change and shift. We all know we could have done some things better. To chastise ourselves by dwelling upon our natural, human actions does not make anything better; but it does slow up the process of getting our deep feelings back in balance. We cannot turn the clock back and do anything differently. We should try to look at ourselves now and then through the eyes of the one who has died, realizing that if consciousness survives it understands and forgives in a way that could not have been possible before.

Don't Drug Yourself

When a painful situation develops, it is not unusual for others to try to ease our pain by giving us pills, drugs, stimulants or tranquilizers. But such things only postpone the facing of our grief. They momentarily take the sharp edge off our feelings, leaving in exchange a dull ache for a longer period of time. This interference with the natural expression of anguish at the loss of a loved one is harmful. Unless the circumstances are most unusual, it is wise to resist the impulse to ease discomfort in that way.

Don't Feel Sorry for Yourself

Of all emotions, self-pity leads the list in pure futility. You have seen people faced with despair who react by making mental lists of every possible bad thing that could ever happen to them or the world. They pile despair on despair.

It does no good. It makes you feel worse, and you already are unhappy enough. It distorts your thinking so that the good looks small and the bad looms menacingly large. When you catch yourself slipping into that kind of thinking, put the brakes on, for you are going down grade, and will have to work that much harder to bring yourself up again.

Don't Run Away

If some well-meaning person says, "You need a long trip. Just get away from it all," don't let yourself be fooled. The you that has been injured by acute loss is the same you that would go with you on the journey. The best place to face readjustment is where the readjustment must finally be made. There is a time and a place for rest and change, but there is no rest or change when you are running away from something you must squarely face. Face it, resolve it and then you can truly find new sources of inner strength in change.

Don't Withdraw Yourself

Few persons are able to live like hermits, and those who can are not normal. We need friends and relatives to help us keep in contact with the world we live in. Those who withdraw and become emotional recluses are cutting off one of the best sources of strength and help in meeting the future. Sometimes a special effort is necessary before we can mingle with others, but it can be done through social or religious groups, and it helps to restore a healthy perspective to life.

Don't Pay Too Much Attention to What Others Say

We can assume that most people speak with good intentions, trying to be helpful. But they are bound by their own experience, and their experience may not apply to yours. Thus they may say, "It must have been God's will" or "It is better this way," when you know that it is far from being "better this way."

At such times it is hard to find the right thing to say, and in fumbling for words many persons say ill-considered things. Make allowances for such statements, and try to understand that sympathetic feelings go with them even though the words distress you.

Don't Cross Bridges Until You Come to Them

You may be overcome with uncertainty and apprehension about the future. You may wonder what will become of you and others dependent upon you. Don't try to make important decisions while you are off balance. Don't anticipate problems. Wait a bit and take care of the immediate, urgent tasks. Get your perspective, look at things when you are calmer, and then determine your assets and liabilities. When you do come face to face with what must be done, you will find the necessary wisdom and strength. There is a solution to every problem. Often it is not a matter of deciding between right and wrong, but which of several right ways would be best for you. When you have made a decision, move ahead with confidence, and do not look back with regret.

Above All, Don't Underestimate Yourself

In the face of major adjustments, many persons fail to recognize their own powers. Each new experience can call forth new abilities and resources.

Do the best you can, and you will be able to say with others who have been through the same experience, "I don't know where the strength came from, but I am surprised at myself. I have done better than I ever expected I could do."

HOW GRIEF IS RELIEVED

GRIEF RELIEVES ITSELF EVENTUALLY, but it takes its own course, and sometimes the course is slow.

The separation caused by death is an emotional amputation. When I visited amputees in a military hospital, they described strong sensations in the parts of their bodies that were no longer there. The nerve system of the leg was gone, for example, but the nerve connections in the brain were still able to "feel" pains in the toes! In time, that part of the brain adapted itself to the absence of the leg. Then the sensations ceased. But this did not occur at once; it was a slow process, set to nature's deliberate time schedule.

A woman once asked me, "How can they go on with everything as if nothing has happened? Doesn't anyone know that Tom just died?" Her feelings were so intense that she could not accept the fact that the world did not share them. But as time went on, she came back into the world with its tasks and problems, and her inner world was gradually restored. It requires hard work to bring into balance the conflict between the inner world of emotional need and the outer world of facts that must be faced.

Your grief will be eased if you can express your feelings. If you want to cry, then cry. If you want to protest against the injustice of life, do so. It is better to "let your feelings go" than to bury them deep, where they can fester or eat away at you. Face the full pain of your loss, for your pain is not only deep—it is healthy. It means that you are alive. That is why it is not a humane act to give sedatives to relieve the acute edge of suffering. To give temporary relief from pain and thereby to prolong its effects is not a kindness. It is easier to deal with the effects when people around you are aware of what is happening and why. Months later, the delayed reactions will not be as clearly understood or as sympathetically handled by the bereaved person or those around him.

It is important to acknowledge the "plusses" of life as well as the "minuses." The woman who committed suicide when one of her children died—and who thus left four others motherless—was emotionally ill. Her act was evidence that her balance sheet of life was not accurately kept.

Nothing helps to restore balance as much as getting to work with something useful and creative. As anyone knows who has ever ridden a bicycle, it is difficult to keep balance while standing still, but

forward motion makes it possible to maintain
balance with ease. So it is with life itself. When up-
setting events tend to get life off its course, work
helps right it again.

When your mind is thus diverted for increasing
periods of time, do not feel disloyal to the one you
loved and lost because your thoughts have turned
to other things. Do not feel guilty if your attention
strays. This process is natural and leads eventually
to "letting go" of the past and to the gradual, inevitable turning toward the future. It is unnatural
only when we cannot continue to live and think of
anything but our loss.

When grief produces a state of emotional im-
balance that persists, the bereaved person may be
in need of special help and understanding. If,
after a few days, a person acts as though he has lost
contact with reality, is unable to care for his own
basic needs, and fails to give proper consideration
to the needs of others, he may be in need of help.
But before you make a self-diagnosis or try to tell
someone else he is behaving abnormally, think about
it carefully. The conditions you observe may cor-
rect themselves quickly. Sometimes the normal looks
abnormal for short periods of time while acute
distress exists.

WHEN GRIEF
GETS OUT OF HAND

MOST PEOPLE HAVE MORE INNER STRENGTH than they recognize in themselves. They can survive the most trying conditions. A mother with a sick child can stay up night after night and draw on a reserve of stamina that is truly amazing. Most persons meet the unusual stress of grief by using this reserve power.

But some of us can stand less stress than others, and may come apart at the seams emotionally. When this happens it is distressing to the person affected, but often even more so to those who see what is happening and want to do something to remedy it.

In order to meet these unusual circumstances it is important to know three things.

First, what is happening? Let us make a comparison. What causes a person to break a leg? Unusual stress is put on the leg, and so it gives at the weakest point or where the stress is greatest. Sometimes it is a green-twig break, where only part of the bone gives away. Or it may be a simple fracture, where the break is complete but the bone springs back when the pressure is off. Or it may be a compound break, where damage is done to the tissue around the bone.

Whichever kind of break it is, it is caused by unusual stress. There are healing forces that can help restore the leg to full use. Part of the healing force is in the bone itself, in the blood and repair equipment of the tissue. Part of the healing force is supplied by the physician who sets the bone and puts it in a cast so that it is protected from further stress until it heals. Part of the healing process is the rest and freedom from stress that is given the patient while the bone knits.

Something like this happens to emotions when they are put under more stress than they can take. Just as a person cannot walk with a broken leg, so a person with fractured, smashed emotions has a difficult time getting along. He has inner resources that will help the healing, but he may need an expert at setting fractured feelings; and he needs protection from the kind of stress that makes things worse rather than better.

A fractured feeling is different from a broken bone in some ways, but very similar indeed in others. Each comes from a specific cause; each can be healed; and each calls for special consideration during the healing process. Understanding is part of the special consideration. A broken bone is easily recognized, but it is not easy to recognize the significance of emotional outbursts or lack of response in a bereaved person.

So the second question that follows naturally is, How can we recognize abnormal symptoms?

You may be wondering whether your feelings are normal. You may be wondering about other members of the family or group who express their grief in ways that trouble you. You expect them to be sad and to weep, but when a bereaved one sinks into such a state of depression that his color changes and he is unable to care for his own physical needs for many days, then his expression of grief may be considered somewhat abnormal. This also applies to anyone showing elation, extreme anxiety or sharp anger. Sometimes persons suffering in this way are suspicious of everyone—especially the doctor, the funeral director, the spiritual leader or a close friend. Also he may withdraw in silence and be unable to communicate with anyone.

The third question is, What can we do about it?

Usually the best help comes from the persons in the community who have been trained for this task. The clergyman is often able to help resolve feelings of grief. At other times, the family physician is helpful. Funeral directors have had long experience helping people with grief. The services of a psychiatrist or a psychologist can be beneficial since they work primarily with mental and emotional states.

When all these forces work together, human and natural, the suffering individual is restored to health of body, mind and spirit. To be sure, he has scars that will never entirely disappear, but he is whole again and prepared to move into the future with greater confidence and inner stability.

HOW TO HELP
A GRIEVING CHILD

THE CHILD'S REACTION TO GRIEF is different from ours and should have special understanding.

In the first place, his experience is limited. He must fit each new event of life into the limited past he has lived through. Most of the things he has wanted we have been able to give him. Unless he is old enough to have learned to accept deprivation when we say "no" about relatively small things, he will be desperately resistant when a big "no" comes along in the form of the death of someone he loves.

His reaction will also depend upon his previous ideas about death, and the explanations he has received about dead birds or animals.

Most of all, however, he will be influenced by the expression of feelings of the adults around him. If he encounters only hysteria and collapse and nagging recrimination, he will naturally be overwrought and frightened, because in addition to his own feelings of loss he is suffering the panic of seeing grown-ups go to pieces. If a family talks with composure, explaining to children in a language they can understand that someone they loved is not going to be there any more, the child accepts the quiet expression and responds in similar fashion.

The problem of helping the child is complicated, since there are so many kinds of death, and since children of various ages differ in their reactions.

When an elderly person dies, it is simple to explain that if the body is worn out, the person has no more use for it. His spirit leaves it, just as we move out of a house when it is too old to live in any longer. A child of any age can accept that. He may be helped to grasp the idea of a spiritual world where bodies are no longer needed.

When a young person dies, especially a parent,

it becomes more difficult to explain—partly because there is no satisfying explanation and partly because the persons best able to talk with the child are too stunned and grief-stricken to think quickly and speak wisely.

The death of a young parent or a playmate might well plunge a child into panic. Life suddenly becomes unpredictable; the ground is shattered under his feet. Often in ways it is hard for us to understand, the child feels personally responsible for this death. He fears that it was brought on by something he thought or said or did.

Someone must rescue the child, or this loss of faith in the stability of life—this fear that no one, no one at any time, is safe from death—may lead to severe emotional problems in adolescence and young adulthood.

How can we save the child from fear?

When a frightened infant screams we hold him close to us to give him physical reassurance. The same thing can be done mentally and spiritually for the older child who feels that his world is falling away. Some adult whom he trusts must be stable and calm as he talks with the child, convincing the child that no matter how lonely and sad he feels, everything is peaceful and undisturbed for the one who has died. If the adult believes in spiritual survival he can tell the child with conviction that there is another life, where the person who formerly lived in a familiar body can go on living without pain or trouble. After all, our faith assures us that a Creator wiser than we governs the universe. And even though we do not understand all about it, we rest secure in the belief that there is a reason beyond our own that undergirds life.

In the case of an older child, the use of analogies sometimes helps. When a musician is playing a piano, the instrument is "alive" and music comes from it; but when the pianist leaves, the piano is quiet and lifeless. When the person dies, the living being that controlled the muscles, spoke the words and did the deeds goes, and the body lies quiet and unused.

When a young person dies in an accident—either an external mishap or an organic failure of the body—explanations are excruciatingly difficult. We cannot permit the child to come to feel that this is common; we do not want to induce fear and dread in him. And our own grief is so much more searing, so much more devastating, that we even find it hard to speak. But we must. In this situation, I sometimes seek analogies in nature. Sad accidents happen in the world that no one can help. A rosebud—one among many on a bush—is snapped off its stem by a careless passerby. A half-grown bird—one of thousands in the parks or fields—falls from its nest. One young tree is blown over in a storm. We cannot easily explain these events. We just have to endure them. If we believe in the goodness of the creative mind, our idea of God, we know that even the most distressing events can work out for good, for us and for those we love, after death.

That assurance must be given repeatedly. Most children four or five years old can comprehend the feeling of assurance that an adult communicates even if they do not grasp all of the meaning of the idea expressed. If the child does not find this, the emotional ground will quiver under his feet for a long time.

Sometimes a child will open doors for your help by his observations and questions. It is important to be alert to these, for the average adult is apt to over-explain and answer questions that the child is not really asking. Listen closely and you will able to tell what he most needs reassurance about, what he is most interested in, and how much information he can "take."

One five-year-old provided a clue when she asked of her dead father, "Is his mommy there to take care of him?" She desperately needed to know that her father was not lost or lonely. The presence of a mother seemed the ultimate of security to her. She needed some affirmative answer to satisfy her, and at that time this was all she needed.

If the adult believes in God, he should guard against referring to a tragedy as "God's will." Untimely deaths sometimes result from ignorance, willfulness or carelessness on the part of human beings. If a child is led to think that such things are God's will, he is apt to rebel against a deity who would perpetrate such cruelty, and his religious beliefs may be permanently crippled. Or he may feel that God is going to "will" his death next. Such a child may live in absolute dread for weeks or months, without ever giving any clue to his terrors.

When someone who does not believe in spiritual survival tries to give comfort, he will appeal to other inner resources of the child to bear the grief. We live in a world where all living things are born, grow and die. We see it happen in the four seasons. The leaves bud, grow to maturity, wither and fall off the tree. Then life begins again in other buds on the same tree.

Whether a person believes in God or not, he eventually comes to the point, with himself as well as with a child, where death cannot be explained or "after death" described. It must be accepted and the separation borne—whether one is three, seven, fifteen or seventy.

Remember, too, that a child is sensitive to deceit, and that it is no kindness to invent a story that leads him to distrust adults. To tell him that his father has gone on a trip and won't be back for a long time is damaging to the child. He begins to ask himself questions that fit his capacity to comprehend. Why did father go? Why didn't he say good-bye? Is he angry at me? Did I do something wrong that caused him to leave without saying anything?

Feelings of guilt, insecurity, and apprehension flood his mind, and he can't find the answer through a wall of falsehood.

To tell him that his father has "gone to sleep" may harm him even more, since he then might fear to go to sleep himself. He may not understand much about death, but it is better for him to start learning in a

mood of trust and security rather than in a con-
spiracy of deceit and subterfuge that adds further
injury to the grief that is already a large burden for
a small child.

If a child is curious about what takes place at the
funeral home, he may need to go with an adult who
can explain in a quiet, matter-of-fact way what the
funeral director has done. One nine-year-old girl
asked these questions about a neighbor who had
died: "Do they have him standing up? Does he have
his pajamas on? Are his eyes closed?" She was told
that the family wanted to think of him as being very
comfortable, so he was lying down peacefully. They
wanted to remember him as he was before he had
been sick, so he was dressed in his usual clothes.
Even though he didn't need his body any more, he
would want to leave it neat and orderly. A child
should be permitted to visit the funeral home if he
wants to satisfy his mind about questions that are
important to him—but not in the presence of hyster-
ical adults, and not against his will, for it is important to remember that his feelings are worthy of
respect.

People ask about letting children go to the funeral. It is perfectly reasonable for a child to share

the family life during these emotionally-charged days. He may not understand all that takes place at the service, but he should not feel excluded from an experience that is obviously affecting the rest of the family. His wishes should be respected, however; if he does not want to go, it might be damaging to force him to do so.

We know that a child's attention span is short, and that most children can be diverted easily from a morbid state of mind. An effort should be made to give him some activity outside the grieving household, even if it is only a trip to the grocery store. He needs to see the world moving along in its customary manner; he must mingle with people at their habitual tasks. He must hear you respond calmly when someone refers to the death that has occurred in the family.

Remember that what you say and do has a marked effect upon how the child thinks and feels. He is able to share only a small part of your feelings because he has had only a small part of your experience. But as far as they go, his feelings must be valued and carefully treated. He must have something strong and stable to which to cling. He must have something truthful in which to believe. Then, whether he is three or thirteen, he will develop the courage to accept this major change in his life.

THE FUNERAL

*Y*OU PROBABLY HAVE MIXED FEELINGS about the funeral. If it has not yet taken place, you are wondering if you will be able to control your emotions. You have been considering what you should ask the clergyman to read that would have special meaning for the person who has died.

If you are reading this after the funeral has taken place, you realize that the words that were spoken or read brought you reassurance of the spiritual quality of life that is not measured by space or time, and made you aware of that inner kingdom of strength that can be drawn on at such times. You were probably gratified that many friends showed their regard for your loved one by attending the service. They shared your grief.

Feelings, whether under control or not, are "at home" in this service. Everyone knows you are full of sorrow. This is the place where your friends accept your feelings. The community is telling you that any way you express your grief is understood.

The funeral also serves another purpose. It reinforces the fact that death has actually taken place, and that your loved one is gone beyond recall.

If this statement shocks you, remember that there are two kinds of feelings. There are those feelings we know we have. For instance, we know we feel despair at the prospect of never seeing the beloved again, regret over things we did or failed to do, fear of facing the future alone.

But there are other feelings we don't know we have, emotions that lie below the surface like the roots of a tree. One of these is the desire to escape from pain. The only way to escape it is to avoid having it. So, far below the surface, we refuse to believe that something has happened to cause pain.

Often we hear a bereaved person say, "I can't believe it." The doctor has told you that the loved one is dead, but the knowledge must seep into every corner of your being, and that is often a slow, difficult process. "I can't believe it," comes the voice from deep inside. But you must believe it before you can learn to bear it, and the funeral helps you do this.

The events leading up to the service also help to awaken your total being to the truth. The articles in the newspaper, the messages of sympathy, the gathering of friends and relatives, the moments spent quietly with the physical remains—all support the realness of your experience so that no part of you can run away and say, "It really isn't so."

Most community funeral customs are a public recognition of death, and the value to the life of the community of the person who has died. Think of these customs as an expression of concern for you. Think of them as a symbol of the community's grief. Observing these conditions helps you to believe what has happened. The community accepts the truth, and that helps you to accept it, too.

The funeral director is trained to be aware of your needs and to do everything possible to help you face your bereavement. He has had more experience than anyone else in leading persons through these distressing circumstances with patience and understanding. This is what he believes about a funeral:

A funeral must face the reality of death—not avoid it.

A funeral must provide a setting wherein the religious needs of the bereaved may be satisfied.

A funeral must provide faith to sustain your spirit.

A funeral must help free you from guilt or self-condemnation.

A funeral must help you express your feelings.

A funeral must direct you beyond the death of the loved one to the responsibilities of life.

A funeral must, in a personal way, help you face a crisis with dignity and courage.

A funeral must above all provide an environment where loving friends and relatives can give you the help you need to face the future with strength and courage.

The funeral gives testimony that there is a tomorrow. Others, it says, have faced and lived through acute grief, and they point the way for you.

LET YOURSELF BE HELPED

MANY PERSONS WILL COME TO YOU and say, "Please let me know if there is anything I can do." Or they may say, "I want to help, so don't hesitate to call on me."

These persons mean what they say. They share your feelings of loss and know how difficult life is for you right now. They would gladly do anything they can to ease its burdens. It would make them feel better could they do so.

There is no reason why you should not let them. It is good for them and it is good for you. They should not be left with good feelings and good intentions unused. You should have the benefit of their kindness and good will.

Your first inclination might be to say, "Yes, you can do something for me. Please go away and leave me alone with my sorrow." But you won't say that because you know that life must go on, and that these persons are a part of the life you have known and will know again.

There are many things that have to be done. They can be made easier by letting your friends help.

The minister or religious counselor wants to be helpful in easing your grief. He understands such things, for he has worked with many persons with feelings like yours. He is a symbol of the spiritual strength that is available to you now.

The funeral director wants to be a friend. He is dedicated to doing his difficult task so that suffering can be eased. He can make many helpful suggestions. Many of the details can be left to him. That is what he wants to do and you are wise to let him be helpful in ways he has found by experience have proved helpful to others.

There are more practical answers to the question, "What can I do?" You can assign one friend to the telephone and another to the task of answering the doorbell. You can let another take over the chores in the kitchen. You can have another one make a car available for errands. Others may be given baby-sitting or child-care tasks, or they can act as companions for the aged. Others may furnish accommodations for out-of-town visitors. These things will all be necessary, and you do a favor to your friends when you give them a chance to put their good feelings to work for you. For them, it takes the place of words they don't know how to say.

When the first few days are over there are other ways you need help. A lawyer, a real estate man, an insurance man and a banker may have been among those who offered to help you. To them you could wisely say, "Thank you, I will need your help next week. I'll call on you then."

There are usually legal matters to be attended

to. The average person is lost in legal language and small print. The lawyer can quickly and helpfully guide you, and he is the representative of your interests. He can keep you from doing things that might be to your disadvantage later.

Money is always a problem. Funds may be tied up temporarily. A banker can make suggestions that will help you arrange your financial matters wisely and well. That is his business and he is glad to give you his services at such a time.

Death often involves insurance. Most persons need insurance funds promptly in time of crisis. This is such a time for you, and the insurance company's representative will help you with the problems you face.

Sometimes in settling an estate, real property is involved. Here the guidance of a trusted real estate person can be helpful in saving time, energy and money.

When your friends and family are near you, force yourself to perform a task that you may possibly fear. Begin to do what must be done with the personal objects we all leave behind us. Certainly your emotions will be open to hurt and bruise and pain; but more so if you keep putting all this off to the future. Persons who say after weeks or years, "Her room is just as she left it," are storing up problems for the future. They are still saying, "I don't believe it." Eventually they must believe it; and they will do less damage to themselves and others if they start now. Steel yourself for the task and take care of the small things at once. Someone can make good use of the shoes and clothing. Go through pockets for crumpled hankerchiefs and gloves, small change and trinkets. It is better to find them now than to come upon them unexpectedly several weeks from now. The will may specify what is to be done with major possessions—but this small, intimate currency of daily living should not be left to tangle your emotions in the days to come. Do this now, when friends are with you to help you and help you remember. Talk now, cry now, face life now with their loving support.

Often the community has resources to help its members meet personal problems that arise. The larger the community the more varied its services will be. These may range from personal counseling to employment advice, from day nursery services to facilities for senior citizens. These resources are available to you, and you can help yourself by letting them help you.

Some persons are uncertain about government services, considering them impersonal and tangled with red tape. This is far from the truth. The representatives are people like you and like me, most often doing their work with understanding and a desire to be helpful. Matters having to do with insurance, taxes or Social Security can be taken to them directly, and genuine helpfulness will usually be shown toward you and your problems.

One of the reasons why death is such a shock to those who must carry on is that it brings many practical problems of adjustment and reorganization to life. It is important to know that the persons around you are ready and willing to help in meeting these problems, whether it be the neighbor down the street or the representative of the Social Security Board.

It is also well to remember that other persons who have gone through your experience have been helped by others, perhaps by you yourself, and that they now want to pass on to you some of the kindness shown them. And as you learn from your experience, you will be better able to do the same thing for others a month, six months or six years from now.

That is how life goes on in the community. Helpfulness is a resource we all draw on. It is also a reservoir into which we pour our understanding and good will. Don't hesitate to draw on it as you need it, and contribute to it as you are able.

FACING THE FUTURE

*A*FTER WE HAVE GONE THROUGH the first pain of grief, and have summoned all our strength for the days of public encounter and private family activity, we come to a time that may be even more difficult.

Relatives return home. Friends go back to the normal routine of their days. They greet us in friendly fashion but they do not speak again of the loss that is aching so freshly in our minds.

We return to our quiet duties, knowing that we must. Yet we are not quite the same. Our world is not the same, either. We have new problems to face, new ways of living to accept. How well will we perform these important tasks?

A few days ago we had many friends and relatives around who were sincerely offering help—but then there were really few tasks to be done. Now there are many things to be done. We don't quite know where to begin. We have to face them with little or no help. A new feeling of aloneness comes over us.

You may have to learn how to live as a widow with a variety of personal and financial problems. You may have to face a complex mass of legal documents and conferences. Or you may have to try to solve the problems of caring for motherless children, or for an elderly person who is alone after many years of close companionship. You may have new and burdensome responsibilities, or you may have a vacant spot in the home where a time-consuming daily task is now ended.

All of these things are a part of the adjustment to living when death occurs. Facing the future is not easy, but it can and must be done.

What are some of the simple things we can keep in mind as we meet these new days and their problems?

First, it is wise to move slowly when making important decisions that cannot be reversed. **Time** gives perspective, and the passing of the days **makes** it possible to see more clearly what is important **and** what is not.

Many persons have lived to regret decisions made hurriedly. A home sold quickly at a sacrifice, a decision to live with one's children and in-laws, a move to another part of the country—these can be quite different in their effect from what was originally expected. The old home, the old associations and the familiar part of the country can be stabilizing forces in life. They can give you something you need emotionally that cannot often be forthcoming from strangers or even from those whom you know well but who are busy with their own lives and problems.

Second, you must keep a growing edge on life. An American poet was asked on his eightieth birthday how he kept young in spirit, and in answer he pointed to a cherry tree in blossom, asking in turn, "Where are the blossoms?" The answer was, "On the new wood." It is the young branches that have the blossoms and bear fruit. The tree keeps its life by growing new life.

An elderly widow in despair kept asking her doctor, "But what can I do?" He answered, "Why don't you learn to paint?" She took him seriously, learned how to paint, found a new interest, new friends, and a whole world she had not known before in museums and galleries. She grew some "new wood" and it blossomed for her.

As you reluctantly turn your eyes from the past to the future you can do it more easily if you seek new interests, new knowledge, new friendships, new experience—yes, new life.

Third, don't let bitterness or grudges invade you. The time of grief can easily become a time for resentment. Persons do things, or neglect to do things, and we say to ourselves, "I'll never forget that." But it is wise to make every possible effort to forget such abrasions. When your emotions are worn thin it is quite natural that you will be more sensitive and thus more easily hurt. But resentment is a heavy load to carry, and it doesn't do anybody any good.

Someone has pointed out that grudges are like a bag of stones carried on our shoulders, never to be set down. They become heavier with the passing of the years, as our strength lessens. If we add still more grudges, the bag becomes so heavy that we stagger under its weight. It is sad to see a person bent double by a back-breaking burden he does not have to carry. A bit of insight and understanding and a willingness to forgive quietly and forget quickly make it possible to set the burden down and walk with lighter step into the future.

Fourth, be kind to yourself. You have to spend a lot of time with yourself. You have to listen to what you say to yourself. You have to put up with yourself in all the ways that are. So be kind to yourself.

Often we hear persons say, "He is his own worst enemy." We know what that phrase means. Frequently an individual judges himself more severely than he would another. He demands more of himself than he would of others. He says things to himself that he would not like others to say. He criticizes himself and condemns his actions when he would be understanding of the same behavior in another. In fact, he makes life so miserable for himself that he would be angry at anyone else who dared do the same things to him.

This happens because there may be a civil war going on inside of you, the sort that develops when there is conflict between the person you are and the person you think you would like to be. Or there may be an uneasy peace between what you think of yourself and what you expect others to think of you. There may be open warfare between your kindly self and your demanding self. And you are in the middle.

Now is a good time to say, "I've had enough of this." Life is too short to waste in self-damage. We need all of our energy to move ahead and face the future. So sign a peace treaty within yourself, and determine from now on to make it a primary obligation to be kind to yourself. It may be difficult at first, but try. It will be worth it.

RELIGIOUS RESOURCES FOR FACING GRIEF

*T*HE MAJOR RELIGIONS OF MANKIND have helped the grief-stricken face the emotional crises of life. They have done it by meeting three needs: the need for perspective in life; the need for spiritual values in measuring life; and the need for inner strength on the part of the bereaved person.

You know how easily a strong emotion can move things out of focus. We speak of a person becoming "blind with rage," just as we say that "love is blind." We know that strong emotion can start a chain reaction that distorts circumstances and ignores cold facts. The person who is not involved wonders why the emotionally overwrought cannot see what should be quite plain. Yet under the same emotional conditions he would be apt to react the same way. When such circumstances overcome life, something is needed to restore clear vision.

Religious institutions have always sought to do this. In the midst of time they point to the values that are timeless. In the midst of distressing circumstance they seek to emphasize the rest of life as the adequate setting within which tragic events take their proportional place. Life then becomes the measure of its tragic events, rather than the tragic incidents being the measure of life.

The traditional processes of worship—with their beautiful surroundings, the art forms of literature, poetry and music, and the invitation to be calm in the presence of the symbols of eternal things—speak directly to the inner man. The events of yesterday are seen differently in the light of man's long struggle to deal with such events. In worship the person can be alone with his deepest thoughts while yet surrounded by and supported by others who share a common heritage and a similar spiritual concern.

The quiet serenity of a place of worship works

its gentle healing as the person's inner tumult is stilled and the turbulent emotions are calmed by the reassurance of eternal things.

When someone near to you dies, one of the important functions of the religious group is to help you refocus your thinking on the values that death cannot destroy. Sometimes this is done by the promise of a continued life of the spirit. Sometimes it is done by directing the mind to contemplate the acts of life that live on after the physical phase of experience is over. You need only look about to see reminders of life's continuing influence. Beethoven still lives in his music. Shakespeare lives on in his drama. Roebling lives on in the Brooklyn Bridge, and Mark Twain lives on in the characters he created. So it is that parents live on in their children. "The works that men do live after them."

Because the religious group is dedicated to creating values and keeping them alive in the minds and spirits of men, it is quite natural for the religious institution to try to enrich memory. All the great religions have rituals through which the lives of the dead are brought again to memory, and the values they treasured are commended to those who live after them.

Perhaps your religious group makes its most

significant contribution to your need by helping to strengthen your faith when it is sagging under the stress of tragic events. With a firm belief that behind the events of life there is a meaning and purpose that reflects the law and order of the universe, you meet life's circumstances "sustained and soothed by an unfaltering trust."

Religious teaching recognizes the mystery of life. The elements of true mystery become more mysterious the more we know of them. So with life, the more we know the more we are aware of the fact that we know little or nothing about the origin or final end of life except as it is made known to us through our religious faith. In times of crisis this faith becomes unusually important.

Death is a great mystery. It challenges our thinking and imagination. What we feel about death tends to shape what we feel about life. If death is a blotting out of all there was of an individual, then the value of life itself decreases. But if death is like another birth, where new possibilities for an emerging life continue, life is enhanced.

Religious teaching, rooted as it is in ages past, helps us feel related to things that remain amidst change. The ancient wisdom that has nourished the souls of men through untold generations still speaks to your need.

If you are actively related to the life of a religious group you will find it has deeper meaning for you now than before, for one of its purposes is to sustain life in times of crisis. If you have not had any connection with a religious group, you may find a strength there now that you had not imagined. As one man put it who had never participated in religious activity but heard the reading of the Twenty Third Psalm at a funeral service, "That is good. It is talking right at me."

Religion helps a person to look up and out and not down and out. It helps him to give expression in living to a faith that is not measured by physical life alone. It ties him to eternal things when he needs them most. It is not without reason that the community entrusts the care of the bereaved to the religious leaders of its group life. Their experience with life and death, their understanding of people, and their own faith make them valuable to us when we seek to emerge from the depths of our grief.

Do not deny yourself the help and strength a religious point of view can place upon your sorrow.

STRENGTH
FOR THE SORROWFUL

*A*S WE BRING TO A CLOSE these thoughts about you and your grief. I would like you to become philosophical for a few moments.

A wise teacher once said, "Blessed are they that mourn for they shall be comforted." These words are a paradox, but truth often is found in the paradoxical. Sorrow and comfort are opposite extremes. Yet wisdom invites us to look carefully at sorrow, for in it are the roots of true meaning for life.

The one who spoke those words did not say that sorrow was good, but he did indicate that it is so much a part of life that we do not really begin to live until we have learned the high art of dealing with sorrow creatively. What he meant was that we can create something good from sorrow if we will.

Some persons are destroyed by sorrow. They let it make them bitter and disillusioned. It destroys their faith in everything.

Others are made strong through the wise handling of their grief. They gain new sensitivity and deep, rich faith. They develop understanding and more genuine sympathy for others.

Until we can handle our sorrow and grief wisely and well, we will not come to terms with life. The mysterious change brought about by mourning is not so much a concern with externals as an achievement of a quality of living. It is not unbridled grief but healing, building sorrow.

What can this creative handling of sorrow do for you?

Sorrow can bring perspective to life. An understanding of life grows out of a realization of its tragic nature as well as its great joys. Just as drama reaches its highest expression in tragedy, so also life achieves its most sublime expression when we master tragedy.

How can we know true happiness without a basis for contrast? Rembrandt knew how to use shadow for that purpose. His paintings reflect insight and meaning not because they are daring in their use of color, but rather because light is used sparingly, and in strong contrast with the shadows from which it emerges.

Centuries ago a woman in grief went to Buddha to plead for the return to life of her child. Buddha sent her away to collect a bowl of peppers from families who had known no similar grief. He promised to minister to her need when she returned at the end of her quest. However, when evening came she returned with an empty bowl and a heart filled with new understanding.

Grief can bring new understanding of self, and richer sympathy for others. When we seek only comfort we seek the meaningless. There is no knowledge of comfort until we have been uncomfortable.

Sorrow can bring security if we learn to let go of what we cannot and should not cling to. We have seen that our very human self-centeredness is an important ingredient of bereavement. It is unrealistic and illusory to cling to the past. Such an attitude destroys the present and jeopardizes the future. Creative sorrow knows how to let the past be past because it has found a larger reality within which past experience takes its proper place.

The inability to let go is rooted in immature emotions. The child clings to a Teddy bear or a worn toy for security. The adult with immature emotions clings futilely to the illusions of life. He refuses to let go because he has no mature basis for satisfying his needs. Maturity brings the deep inner comfort that grows with the ability to adjust oneself to reality. Then the inner life remains secure, for it becomes master of external circumstance instead of being mastered by it.

This inner security comes from a knowledge of deep inner sources of strength that respond to the evidence of order and stability in all of the rest of creation. This knowledge makes one aware of the fact that he is never alone, but is part of something infinitely greater than himself.

Doubt as the opposite of faith creates unreasoned fear. The fearful soul dies a thousand deaths, while the soul that is rooted in faith never fully dies. For the strength of faith is like the strength of life.

Faith does not operate on the immature promise of seeking what we want in life as much as it seeks to make something fine of what life brings to us. It knows the importance of creative adjustment to the circumstances we do not make but must accept.

Religious faith is far more than an opiate against the sorrow of life. It is an incentive toward more and better experience in living.

"Blessed are they that mourn for they shall be comforted." In this paradox sorrow is not commended. It is recognized as inevitable. We are shown that we must learn to use sorrow creatively, that true happiness can come only when the spirit reaches maturity, that sorrow may hasten the spirit's growth to the place where it gains a mature perspective on the incidents of life—a capacity to let go of illusions and hold on to spiritual truth, and to know the positive power of a sustaining faith.

We might say it this way: "Blessed are those who use their sorrow creatively for they shall find a security that is not shaken by circumstance, but rather produces the fruits of enriched sympathy, heightened understanding and deepened faith."